Reminiscences of Dr. F.J. Pond

The Penn State Campus
in the Atherton Era

Reminiscences
of Dr. F.J. Pond

The Penn State Campus
in the Atherton Era

Nittany Valley Press

Copyright © 1942 Dr. Francis J. Pond

Published in the United States of America
by Nittany Valley Press
nittanyvalley.org

ISBN: 978-0-9853488-3-0

Pond, Dr. Francis J.
Reminiscences of Dr. F.J. Pond

Cover Photograph © 2012 Hannah Lane
Courtesy of Onward State

Second Edition

Contents

Reminiscences of Dr. F.J. Pond
September 1942

Dr. Francis J. Pond

Dr. Francis J. Pond was born in Holliston, Massachusetts, on April 8, 1871, the son of Abel and Lucy A. Jones Pond. He married Nellie Olds of Circleville, Ohio, on June 10, 1902, and they had the following children: Catherine Olds (deceased), Elizabeth Olds, and Nathan Jones. Dr. Pond received his preliminary education in Holliston, then entered The Pennsylvania State College in September 1888, and was graduated in the chemistry course with the class of 1892. While in college he was an associate editor of the Free Lance from April 1890 to March 1891; assistant editor of the class annual, the La Vie, for 1892; Vice President of the Washington Literary Society for 1890, and its Treasurer for 1891. He was always interested in sports, especially football, and eagerly followed every game.

After a year's post graduate work in chemistry at State, he served a year as instructor in Qualitative and Quantitative Analysis. In October 1894, he entered the University of Göttingen, Germany, and in February 1896, received the degree of M.A., and Ph.D., magna cum laude. After a six months' course at the Royal Mining Academy of Freiberg, Germany, he returned to The Pennsylvania State College on a salary of $800 as instructor in Assaying and Chemistry from 1896 to 1901. When Dr. Ihlseng left, he was asked to take over the entire mining department and was made Assistant Professor of Chemistry and Metallurgy, from 1901 to 1903. During this period he also worked in the Chemistry Department under his brother, Dr. Gilbert G. ("Swampy") Pond. In 1903 he became Assistant Professor of Engineering Chemistry at the Stevens Institute of Technology. In 1906 he was promoted to Associate Professor of Chemistry, and in 1909 to Professor of Chemistry. For many years he was head of the Chemistry Department at the institution. In 1907 he was made Dean of Freshman, which position he also held a long time. He was a member of Sigma Chi, Tau Beta Pi, Phi Kappa Phi, and the American Chemical Society. He has many articles to his credit and revised and greatly enlarged Hensler's "Terpenes", the American edition being called "Chemistry of the Terpenes."

Dr. Pond died suddenly from a heart attack February 18, 1943, at his home in Upper Montclair, New Jersey. When the following notes were dictated, his accuracy about details and dates of over fifty years ago was observed over and over again.

He also had a nice sense of humor; and during his two weeks' vacation in the fall of 1942, when he spent part of every day reminiscing, he was enjoyed by every one with whom he came in contact.

Transportation

The Buffalo Run Railroad operated as far as Struble's Station. The students used to walk through the woods and get the train at Krumrine's Crossing, northwest of town. In 1892 the railroad was extended from Struble's Station, at the west end of the village, into the college, and the first train came in in April 1892.

One could go by the bus from the Hotel to Lemont and there catch a train from Bellefonte. The train left Lemont about 1:30 in the morning and returned around 2:00 in the afternoon.

When classes went to Bellefonte for banquets etc., they sometimes went in the "Mountain Echo". This bus, capable of holding twenty to thirty people, was hauled by four mules. On both sides was painted the name "Mountain Echo". The driver was Perce Rudy. The Echo was used to carry the students from the Main Building to the Lemont Station at the end of each term and to bring them back at the end of vacation or at the first of the year. It was also used for special trips. For example, the TNE used it every spring to attend the annual banquet down near Penn's Cave. The last time Dr. Pond used the Echo was in 1900 when he took his chemistry classes to Scotia on an inspection Trip.

Campus

When Dr. Francis J. Pond came to school at Penn State in the fall of 1888, he found these buildings: the Main Building; Botany Building and gardens; Experiment Station; President's house; the stone house of the Vice President; Mr. Patterson's house and farm buildings, north of which were the vineyards and orchards; and on the spot where Carnegie Hall now stands were a barn and pig pen. While here at Penn State Dr. Pond saw these additions made: Power Plant, Artesian Well, Electric Light Building, Physics and Chemistry Building, Armory, and four houses for professors. The first class to be held in the new Physics and Chemistry Building was in April 1890.

In 1893 the Engineering Building was completed and was dedicated on February 22nd of that year. That evening a ball was to be held with guests coming from all around. But such a blizzard came up that the train was held up, and some of the guests didn't arrive until mid-night.

Student Accommodations

Most of the students roomed in the Main Building, where they paid a very nominal fee for their room. The college provided an iron single bed, two chairs, a table, and a bureau or stand of some kind. No carpet, curtains, or bedding were furnished. There were usually two students to a room. The fifth floor was the popular place to live during the nineties, probably due to the fact that they were above everybody else and also that a "poke of water" had farther to fall. This "poke of water" was a paper bag filled with water which they dropped down the stairway on some unsuspecting person's head.

John Andy Hunter of the class of 1890 and Bobby Green of the class of 1891 had a telegraph and telephone system respectively. These operated between rooms in the Main Building. This same John Andy had the first gas propelled machine which Dr. Pond ever saw. He had it rigged up and running around Beaver Field at a Penn State game.

A few students were allowed to board themselves, and for their use a few rooms in the Main Building were laid out as kitchens. Most of the students ate at boarding clubs which were run by a student who was working his way through college. The cost per week ranged between two and three dollars; the club charging three dollars was considered a "tony" club. These clubs had various names including Delmonico, Duquesne, Clover, etc.

Faculty Accommodations

In 1896 after Dr. Pond's return from Germany he lived in an apartment above the Post Office on the west corner of College Avenue and Pugh

Street. The apartment included three bedrooms, a dining room, living room, and kitchen for which he paid $23 a month, and this included heat and light.

Guest Accommodations

Guests coming to State College stayed at the University Inn, which was located where the University Club now is. This inn was built by subscription in 1893 and 1894 but never proved much of a success financially. Among other accommodations it provided a dance hall where many of the college dances were held. Around 1896 Phil Foster was proprietor of the inn. In May 1903, the inn burned down and was not rebuilt.

Town

On Pugh Street were the homes of Will Foster, the Glenns, Buckouts, McKee, Osborne, and Robert Foster.

Stores

The stores consisted of "Miff" S. Snyder, General Merchandise and Apothecary Shop; W.L. Foster, General Merchandise; Slagle's Grocery Store; Markle's Butcher Shop, where steak could be bought for 14 cents a pound; Thompson's Bakery; and Shaeffer and Sons' Tailor Shop. The drugs in the drug store were dispensed by the physician, Dr. William Glenn. Sam Grieb also sold tobaccos at the hotel where the State College Hotel is now located, and traveling salesmen came around each month going from house to house selling fancy groceries which could not be bought at the local stores. Later on Shaeffer moved to Philadelphia, and Henry Grimm took over the tailor shop; Laird Holmes bought out the Slagle grocery store. When Will Foster built the flat at the corner of College Avenue and Pugh Street, he moved his store into this building, and it was there that acetylene lights were first used in State College.

Football

Some of the early teams had fancy scores in football. At one time Lehigh beat Penn State 106 to 0. Another memorable time Penn State thought they had a very good team. They took a trip down East in the fall of 1899. One of the teams they played was Yale, and they all felt sure of winning the game. However, they were dis-appointed; and when the telegram came to State announcing the results of the game, this is what it said: "Yale 40, State 0. The team played well." The telegram was sent by Kid Biller, Manager, and the words "The team played well" became a slogan around Penn State.

In the early nineties football and baseball were the only games played at Penn State. Football was officially started in 1887 by Linz, Class of

1892. Linz played quarterback on this first team. There was, however, an informal game played with Bucknell back in 1881. In 1887 Penn State played Bucknell two games and won both of them. Prof. Cleaver, who had played on the Dickinson team, coached the Penn State team. In 1922 Penn State played Syracuse, and the night before the game, at a banquet in New York City, the former living members of this team of 1887 had a reunion.

In the early days Penn State had no compunction about using men on their teams who were not even students at the college. George Bush of Bellefonte, Graham of Phillipsburg, Phil Foster of State College, and Charlie Atherton all played on the team when they were not students in the college. When George Hoskins was here as coach, he played the center position for several years. This playing of a coach was not original with Penn Sate because in the fall of 1890, State played Swarthmore for the first time in its history on what became Beaver Field; in this game one of the ends on the Swarthmore team was "Doc" Shell, who was champion amateur wrestler of the state of Pennsylvania at that time, and he was also athletic coach at Swarthmore. Hoskins came here in 1892. He was a hard worker and gave a lot to the early teams. The fellows all liked him because he wasn't above having a game of penny ante with them occasionally. From here he went to Western University of Pennsylvania (now Pittsburgh) and from there to Bucknell.

While at Bucknell, Penn State protested the playing of Christie Mathewson on the Bucknell team in the fall of 1899 on the grounds that he had played professional football the preceding summer. Bucknell went ahead and played him, and the State team was told to lay for Mathewson, which they did. They were quite angry by this time. When later on in the game Joe Ruble touched the ball down and kicked it in instead of carrying it in, the Bucknell team protested the play and the game ended in a dispute. Coach Hoskins later remarked to Dr. Pond that if any other team but State had protested, they might have accepted the protest; but that he knew that Penn State had for years played men who were ineligible.

After George Hoskins left, the college hired a man the name of Dr. Newton as coach, but for some reason or other the students did not take to him; and the team under the leadership of Max Curtin, who was captain, fired Newton and got Charlie Atherton to act as coach. However, as Newton had been hired by the board, he was re-tained, and the following year things went better. Dr. Newton was the man to develop the place-ment kick. He later went to Lafayette and Lehigh.

The next coach was Sammy Boyle, a man who was so nervous he couldn't watch his team play. Under him, Earle Hewitt made his famous touch-down against West Point which won the game for Penn State.

The year Lehigh beat State 106 to 0 the team had made an eastern tour. They played Lafayette (24-0) on Saturday and had the weekend off, play-ing Lehigh on Monday. They had no training in those days, and the boys returned worn out and in no condition to play. In addition to that they saw blocking and interference used for the first time, and they didn't know how to meet it. When they returned from the trip, the team got off the bus at Sauerstown, the eastern end of College Avenue, and came into town by foot so they wouldn't meet anyone.

In the fall of 1890 State played The University of Pennsylvania for the first time. "Pope" Hildebrand was a star on that team while his opponent was Bowser, a star for Pennsylvania. Both men were big and they had a very noted battle.

In the fall of 1891 State played Bucknell, and the State boys had put up money to bet on the game. At the end of the first half the score was 6-0 in favor of State, but in the second half Bucknell forged ahead and won the game 12-10. Times were hard in State College for a while after that.

In the early years about 1892-1899 football was so rough even "kneeing" was allowed, and the boys on the team were fed cocaine pills to give them stamina. This was a bad habit and resulted in at least one known death.

In those years there was no visible means of support for the football teams, and sometimes in order to make their scheduled trips, the teams had to borrow money from the professors or merchants to finance their journeys. Finally, in 1899 it was decided to put athletics on a more permanent basis, and an athletic fee of $5.00 was charged each student giving him membership in the Athletic Association and admitting him to all games. Dr. F.J. Pond was made Treasurer for this purpose and held this position until 1903 when he was succeeded by "Mickey" McDowell. This was the forerunner of the graduate manager.

One year Penn State was anxious to beat Princeton. In order to do so they tried to cancel the W. and J. game which just preceded it, but W. and J. refused and were indignant to think that Penn State should even have asked them to do so. During the game which was played at State College Dan Miller had his nose broken, Burns was jumped on while he was down and suffered injuries, and a W. and J. man had his collar bone broken. The referees called the game, but the damage had been done — the State boys were unnerved, and they lost the game to Princeton 12-0.

In 1894, when George Spence was manager of the team, they went to Annapolis. "Big" Fisher was captain of the team, and he and McCaskey had a trick play worked out which they felt would secure the game for them. With this in mind they were led to put up their guarantee for bets on the game. Unfortunately the referee would not permit this play, and the boys from Penn State felt they were doomed. As luck would have it, the game ended a tie, and the boys were saved undue embarrassment.

In 1902 State had a man on her football team by the name of Andrew Smith, whose nickname was Big Indian Smith. He played such good football that the coach of Pennsylvania University approached him with an offer to come to Penn with all expenses paid, provided he came immediately so that he might be eligible to play against Harvard the next year. Smith did this and later became known as "The tramp athlete" because he changed schools in the middle of the term. Scribners magazine wrote up his story, and he had to quit playing with the Penn team. Later he became coach at the University of California, and his teams there were known as the wonder teams.

College Colors

The early colors of Penn State were Pink and Black. In those days they had a yell which went something like this:

Yah, yah, yah. Yah, yah, yeh.
Wish-whack. Pink, black —
P.S.C.

Around 1888, when Penn State played Dickinson on the front campus, as there was yet no athletic field, they gave this yell, and the substitutes of the Dickinson team made a parody of it which went like this:

Yah, yah, hay. Yah, yah, yeh.
Bees wax. Bees wax —
A.B.C.

This so disgusted the boys that soon after they not only changed the college yell but also the colors from Pink and Black to Blue and White, and so they have remained ever since.

Military

Classes at this time met from Monday through Friday. Saturday was used for make-up day, hikes, military punishment, etc. Every day there was military inspection both of dress and also of rooms. If the room was untidy or dirty or shoes needed polishing, the boys got a notice on the military bulletin board. Each such report carried one hour's punishment.

On the front campus were four cannon — two brass ones which had been used in the Mexican war and two steel ones which were used for artillery drill. One of the favorite punishments inflicted upon the boys was to make them polish the brass cannon which were merely ornamental. The boys some times shot off the cannon to celebrate certain events. Dr. Pond and Mickey McDowell, who were among the few Democrats on campus, shot off the cannon to celebrate the election of Pattison as Democratic governor of Pennsylvania.

Military drill for Freshman was held about four times a week. One of the first commandants was Lieutenant Pague, a very interesting man and a favorite with the boys. Following him came Silas Wolfe, who did not make a very good commandant. He was known as the "Bull of the west". The next man was McCaskey, who was an excellent man for the place. He brought with him his brother, who had been on the school ship, Saratoga. He was quite an athlete, had studied medicine and at the time of the Spanish American war enlisted and remained in the army. He later returned to Penn State as commandant. In 1917 Dr. Pond read a description of a parade in the New York Times which stated that "Gabby" McCaskey, who was then Major McCaskey, had led the parade.

At the beginning of the Spanish American war Woodruff of Pennsylvania University tried to organize a regiment of football players to go to war. The boys at State thought this was a novel idea and decided to take a group from here. When Dr. Atherton learned of the plan, he called a meeting and spoke to the boys, telling them that they were not needed in the army as yet and that their part was to stay in school. He concluded by saying that if the time came when they were needed, he would go with them as their leader.

Pranks

The college had a human skeleton which the students called Old John; there was also a skeleton of a mule. The boys decided it would be quite a joke to mount Old John on the mule and usher him on the stage during a chapel service. They brought them through a side door near the front of the platform. Miss McElwain sat next to this door, and one morning at a given signal the door opened while the minister was praying, and by manipulation from above the skeleton with its rider moved on to the stage just in front of Miss McElwain. The spectacle was enough to unnerve anyone, but she never "batted an eye".

On the front campus was a flower bed in which one morning in the spring of 1889 the students found a grave of one of the professors. The tomb stone read:

"Sacred to the memory of 'Pat' (James McKee)
Gone but not forgotten."

Sticking out of the grave was a bunch of excelsior which was to represent the whiskers of the professor.

The boys in Dr. Frear's animal chemistry course feared that they might not pass his examination, so they decided to steal his exam questions. But how to do it was the question. The Doctor lived on the third floor of the Main Building. The boys finally decided that since one of them had a room on the fifth floor immediately above Dr. Frear's, they could lower a boy from the fifth floor into the window on third. Because of his slight build, they selected Tom Glenn, who is still living and attended the 50th class reunion in May 1942. For many years he has been a practicing physician in Bradford, Pennsylvania. They lowered him and then pulled him back up to the fifth floor again. But after going to all this trouble and risking the boy's life, they failed to find the paper on which the exam questions were written.

A group of boys went to Pine Grove Mills to a singing school. With them they took the ingredients necessary for the manufacture of hydrogen sulfide, which they started generating in the middle of the song service. Needless to say the service broke up, and the boys of Penn State made the headlines of the newspapers. The story was also published in the Police Gazette.

At the time of the Johnstown Flood "Calamity" Husser (C.S.) had gone home for a vacation. He failed to come back on time and gave high waters as his excuse for his actions. The faculty failed to believe his story, and he was suspended. His class, that of 1892, bolted an examination and went to play a game of baseball as a retaliation for his suspension. As a result the entire class was suspended and they went out in the fields near University Inn and pitched tents. They called the encampment "Camp Suspension." It was several days before the college realized the truth of the flood and took any steps to reinstate the class just as they were beginning to fear that they might not be taken back. One of the members wrote an article entitled "Hickory shingles". They were finally reinstated through the efforts of Dr. J.A. Beaver.

The first cane rush was in 1888. The idea was to see which class could get the most hands on the cane. This was later discontinued, and a football game was played instead because they decided a cane rush was too dangerous.

There was a small pool of water, rather more than a pool, very close to the stone house which was then known as the Vice President's house; it was a depression there which evidently had been some sort of a cave in the limestone formation. This was called "the frog pond." In the spring term some of the boys in Dr. Pond's class took a boy, a member of the Fow Tpsilon Tset Fraternity, from the class below which was the A Prep, and threw him into this frog pond. The boy who got the ducking was named Greer, and he was the son of a Judge Greer of Pittsburgh, Pennsylvania; his brother, Dr. Robert Greer, was later a student of State College and graduated in the class of 1895.

Religious Life
Churches

There were two churches in town, one a Methodist and the other a Presbyterian. Both were located on College Avenue near the East Gate to the Campus.

Chapel

Compulsory chapel services were held each morning of the week in the Main Building under the direction of a member of the faculty. This rotated, each professor using the service of his own church. The service consisted of a Scripture reading, a song, and a prayer, the boys standing for the song and prayer. The students liked having Josiah Jackson as leader because he was a Quaker and the spirit never moved him to pray, so the students could sit down with bowed heads which gave them more time to study. These chapel exercises came at eight o'clock every morning of the week. On Sunday, Chapel was at nine o'clock in the morning and church at three o'clock in the afternoon. The Sunday exercises were conducted by neighboring ministers. Rev. Lowry, Scotch Presbyterian from Bellefonte and Rev. White from Milroy were frequent visitors.

At first Chapel was held in a room on the second floor front of the Main Building (1888), but by Christmas 1889 the chapel on the first floor was completed, and the second floor room became a library and continued to be so used until The Carnegie Library was built. In chapel the classes were seated in order with the seniors in the front rows. On leaving Chapel the seniors passed out first, followed by the classes in their order.

When the Chapel was still held on the second floor, it was also used as a classroom by "Boss" Reeves, Professor of German and French, and Business Manager of the College.

The Sabbath Day was strictly observed. The Class of 1892 was seriously reprimanded for desecrating the Sabbath. It happened in this manner. Late on Saturday night the Freshman class placed their class flag on top of the Armory and took down the steps leading up to the roof, thinking that since the next day was Sunday it would be left undisturbed for at least a day. However, the Class of '92 decided not to wait, and immediately upon leaving Chapel they rushed to the Armory, and Charlie Aull, an athletic fellow, succeeded in climbing up to the flag. The sophomores were enabled to do most of this before the freshman arrived on the scene as the freshman were the last to leave Chapel. As soon as they could they dashed to the rescue of the flag and the usual fight ensued. Dr. Atherton, arriving on the scene, thoroughly denounced the boys and immediately sat down and wrote letters to the parents of the boys for breaking the Sabbath Day. The letters, however, did not carry much weight as they were written on the Sabbath Day, which was also considered an improper thing to do.

Rhetoricals

"Sport" Davis, Professor of English, started Public Speaking on every Wednesday evening. Attendance was compulsory for freshman and sophomores. The freshman and sophomores gave recitations, while the juniors gave orations. The juniors were graded on these orations, and those with the best grades for the year were chosen as Junior orators for commencement time.

At one of these Rhetoricals, as they were called, Milton E. McDonnell, a freshman, who later became head chemist for the Pennsylvania Railroad and an exceedingly able man, was to speak. The sophomore class of 1892 decided to give him the razz as it were; not to be daunted by this he continued to speak and the louder the sophomores jeered him, the louder he spoke. Professor Davis lost control of the group, and other professors came running from other parts of the building to see what was the matter. Fortunately, the professors were able to see the funny side of the situation, and the class was not punished for this act.

Literary Societies

One of the factors which played an important part in early college life was the literary societies. This not only afforded a means of training in speaking but also offered about the only social life which the students had. There were two literary societies at Penn State—the Cresson and the Washington. They each had meeting rooms on the fifth floor of the Main Building, each with a seating capacity of about 100, a platform at the front, and a piano. Each organization also had a library which later augmented the college Library. The meetings were held every Friday night at 7 o'clock and lasted about an hour and a half. The meeting was opened by the President and the Vice President gave a Bible reading. Following this there were recitations, orations, and music ending with a debate which had a team of two on each side. Following the debate there was a general debate, and at the very end a critic evaluated the performance. A social intermission of about one half hour followed and then the business meeting was held.

The Washington society compiled a paper each week called the Spectator; the two editors read this paper to the society. This was eagerly awaited by the members mainly because of the jokes about their fellow class mates.

The boys spent much time in the Literary Society reading rooms as they subscribed to many home papers as well as the comic magazines of that period, Puck and Judge. These reading rooms were open to any one.

In Dr. Pond's junior year the two societies had a joint debate at the end of the year; Brewer, Hile, and Pond for the Washington Society debated Williamson, Pratt, and Lloyd of the Cresson Society on the question Resolved: That Canada be annexed to the United States. The debate was won by the Cresson Society. One of the judges for this debate was Rev. White of Milroy.

Membership in the Literary Societies was open to any one and there was a great deal of rivalry between the two societies. There were dues of a nominal nature, and they were usually hard to collect. About 1892 or 93 the interest in the literary societies began to wane, probably due to the coming of the fraternities. The Washington Hall later became the Y.M.C.A. rooms and the Cresson was turned into a classroom.

Fraternities and Clubs

The first fraternity at Penn State was the Delta Tau Delta, which was in existence from about 1872 to 1874 when it was eliminated. The second fraternity was the Latin letter society, the Q.T.V. which later became the Phi Kappa Sigma. In 1888 there was formed a Dutch or German letter fraternity, the Fow Tpsilon Tset. This group met in the cellar of the Main Building, and their chief purpose was to control politics and have a good time. The Greek letter fraternities which were organized in 1887 and 1888 were the Phi Gamma Delta and the Beta Theta Pi.

Phi Gamma Delta house was on Allen St. across from where the Post Office now is, and beyond that was the Sigma Chi house. Next were two houses built by a man named Meyers, which he rented for $16.00 a month. Other houses were built by Bert Meek and Harter.

The Adelphi Club was organized about 1893 and was composed of fraternity members. It was a social club and gave several dances during the year, one at commencement time. It disbanded about 1898.

The T.N.E. was a sophomore class fraternity to run politics. They were known for their roughness at initiation ceremonies.

The White Caps was a preparatory organization that was organized about 1888 or '89 for disciplinary measures.

Because there were so few girls in college, the boys who were unfortunate enough not to be found in their graces organized a club known as The 400 Club; the significance of this being that they were above calling at the Women's Cottage.

Music

After Dr. Sparks came, a chapel choir was started in which he and Professor Butz sang. A

Glee Club and Orchestra was organized in about 1890. The college didn't have a band until almost 1900, when Andrew Carnegie, one of the trustees, outfitted a band of which "Patty" Goddard was the first leader. Prior to this there was a band in the village under the leadership of Jim Fulton, who worked on the college farm. He was killed in 1891. The band had rooms in the alley back of College Avenue, and there they met every week.

Dances

There were only three dances a year given to which girls were invited, and then they were mostly imports as there were very few coeds in the school. In between these dances the boys held girless dances. The most famous of these was the masque ball to which no one came who was not masked. This was a yearly event and one eagerly looked forward to. The first ball was given in the Armory in 1890. Prior to that time dancing was prohibited at the college.

Commencement

Commencement was held in the chapel with the faculty sitting on the platform and the seniors in the front seats. The first class to wear the cap and gown was that of 1892, but after that it was discontinued for several years when the custom was again renewed. The faculty did not begin to wear the gown until around 1897. The matter was brought up at a faculty meeting and Dr. Atherton, who had heretofore discouraged the use of it, recommended that it now be adopted because he said that General Beaver had told him as a judge he had worn the gown and felt that it added to the dignity of his office.

As late as 1890 the baccalaureate sermon was given in the afternoon, but after that it was held in the morning. People came for miles around to attend this service. In 1890 the sermon was given by Dr. Atherton himself.

At commencement time an alumni dinner was given in the Armory to graduates and invited guests, and there was always a scramble for tickets to attend this dinner which was free.

Personalities

Dr. Atherton, who was a wonderful man, was also a good politician. He knew how to work the middle against both ends. He went to Harrisburg and secured the first appropriation of any size for the college. This was in 1887 and amounted to $100,000. He also invited inspection tours by the members of the legislature so that they might see for themselves how badly some improvements were needed. This was always a great occasion for the students because a holiday was declared and the boys showed the visitors around and entertained them. It was on one such visit that "Fog-horn" Fow found the heating plant then located in the basement of the Main Building and decided that to have the students living and going to classes above this plant was like living on an active volcano, and he started proceedings which result in the power plant. The heating tunnel was also dug while Dr. Pond was a student at Penn State.

At one time when there was talk of President Atherton's leaving Penn State for another position, the students became perturbed at the rumor. In order to allay their fears, Dr. Atherton spoke to them and explained that he did not intend to leave. He said that he had always felt that institutions were more important than men and his desire for a long time had been to make an institution here at State College, and he did not intend leaving without fulfilling that desire.

The Athertons had a very charming home life. Every day after dinner the family played Whist. The children were all musical, and at one time Charles Atherton led the college orchestra. The other son, Frank, wanted to go to music school, but his father insisted that he first graduate from Penn State. Instead of doing this the boy ran away and joined a traveling orchestra.

Josiah Jackson, a Quaker and an early member of the faculty, was a favorite with the students. He was the father of some of Penn State's illustrious alumni: John Prince Jakson, who was a professor at Penn State; Dugald, a teacher at M.I.T.; and Will Jackson and Helen Jackson, who became Mrs. Louis Reber.

Dr. Armsby was also well liked by the students. He and Dr. Atherton and the Negro barber, Tom DuBois were the only men in State College who wore tall hats. Mrs. Armsby was a gracious woman, and was sometimes referred to as the Duchess of Armsby.

Miss Torrance, a sister of Professor Osborne's was the first librarian. She labored under great difficulties as the library facilities were very poor.

Miss McElwain, the president's secretary, was a very capable woman and well liked by the students. Her sister, Carrie McElwain and Emma Camp were the first women graduates in Civil Engineering. Antoinette Ball was another early coed who made a great impression on the students because of her charming manner.

John M. Ward, "Monte", a Bellefonte boy and later captain of the N.Y. Giants, came to school here. He is alleged to have pitched the first curved ball. It was reported that Professor McKee doubted that a ball could be curved so he put up stakes and Ward pitched the ball around the stakes. In 1908 at the N.Y. Alumni Society banquet John Ward came to the meeting in order to express his esteem for Dr. Buckhout, who was the main speaker of the evening.

Dr. Buckhout was a mild, pleasant, lovable gentleman. He was also so very punctual that one could set a clock by his passing down the street to the college.

John Mitchell, son of the post master, lived opposite the main entrance at Coop corner. He also became a good baseball player and after playing on the State baseball and football teams, he went to Philadelphia and later to the Minneapolis ball clubs. He contracted consumption, however, and died of it as did his sister, Lydia, who was a charming woman.

The Stuart family were also quite prominent around the college. There were Bell, Dan, Margaret, and Elizabeth, who was known as the College widow.

G.G. Pond, L.E. Reber, John Heston, and E.E. Sparks all lived in the Main Building. While residing there, Dr. Pond's small daughter, Millicent, was hit by a snow ball which came through the kitchen window from a snowball fight which was taking place on the front campus. A piece of glass lodged in the snowball and hit the child in the eye, which resulted in the loss of the eye. This was a very tragic incident.

Thomas A. Gilkey, "Dad", paid part of his way through college by acting as college barber. He had his shop on the fourth floor of the Main Building, and the charge for a hair cut was 15 cents.

"Lucy" Linz was instrumental in starting the first football team at Penn State, and he was the first captain. In 1922 he was also instrumental in bringing about a reunion of this team of 1887 in New York City.

J.P. Welch acted as president after Dr. Atherton's death. This was a very critical time because the college was financially embarrassed, and Welch and the faculty did not get along with each other too well. 1896 to 1900 and 1905 to 1908 were two periods of trying times at the college. Funds were scarce, the institution was in debt, and things in general were in a bad state of affairs. In 1906 or

'o7 housing was so scarce that temporary structures were erected to alleviate this condition.
These structures were called the Bright Angel and
the Devil's Den.

John Leete, Assistant Professor in Mathematics
and also registrar was an important figure among
the early faculty. He had a beautiful wife who ac-
cidentally drank poison; but through the foresight
of Dr. Dale of Lemont, a country physician who
was able with his meager supplies to accomplish
wonders, they were able to save her life. They
kept her walking for six hours to pre-vent her
from falling asleep.

Tom Dubois, a colored man, had a barber
shop near Grieb's Motel, and after he left, a white
man took over his business. In 1896 Graham set
up a second barber shop in town and is still here
carrying on a tobacco, candy, and magazine store.

Miscellaneous

In the fall the students were allowed to gather
grapes and fruit from the vineyard and orchard.
They took their pillow cases to carry back their
winter supply of fruit.

In the winter of 1890 the weather was so mild
the dandelions grew in mid-winter.

There were two tragic deaths of students in
the college while Dr. Pond was here. The one was
Patrick, who died in the Main Building of Black

Measles, and the other a boy in the class of 1900, who also died of measles.

The students and children in winter coasted down over the campus, out the east gate, and down College Avenue. They also coasted down the Pugh Street hill.

Dr. Pond came to Penn State from New England and here saw apple butter for the first time. In those days New Englanders were called Yankees, and there was quite a feeling against them. W.P. Rothrock and Pond were roommates in 1889.

Perrine, a man who travels all over the United States visiting the colleges, told Dr. Pond that Penn State had the best equipped electrical engineering laboratory in the United States. He also stated that State College is noted for its enormous rapid growth, beautiful homes, and for the fact that most of its business is done on borrowed money.

There were no class memorials until about 1903.

The students used to make trips down to Penn's Cave. In 1890 when Talbot was on his way to his wedding in Baltimore, he stopped here to see Dr. G.G. Pond. By way of entertainment they hired a carriage and drove down to Penn's Cave.

On the way home the carriage broke down, and they had to walk the rest of the way. Both got a terrific sunburn which greatly embarrassed Talbot because he hated to show up for his wedding in this condition.

Nicknames

Aubie — Abreu, D.
Baldy — Waldron, James H.
Big Indian Smith — Smith, Andrew
Bobby — Green
Bonus — Bohn, W.W.
Buck — Reber, D.C.
Calamity — Musser, C.H.
Chuck — Barclay
Dad —   Gilkey, Tom A.
Dude — Walker, W.H.
Gabby — McCaskey
General —   Hoskins
Granny — Watts, R.L.
Jeffy — Mock
Johnny Pan   — Hamilton, John
Josephus — Weidner
Judy — Rumberger
Levi — Zink
Lucy — Linz
Mam — Camp
Monk —   Suloff
Monte — Ward, John M.
Pete — Meek, George
Rastus — Wieland, George
Rebel — Yocum
Rednose Mike & Colonel — Shields, J.F.
Rosa — Schimer
Rosie — Chamberlain
Sally — Long
Sarah — Swank, Robert
Snitz — Dale, Fred

Sport — Davis, Prof.
Sweetie — Fields, John
Ting-a-ling — Holmes

About Nittany Valley Press

Nittany Valley Press offers a special collection meant to foster a spirit of community across time for Penn Staters, Central Pennsylvanians, and friends. Nittany Valley Press encourages an appreciation for the history, customs, and spirit of Central Pennsylvania's Nittany Valley, the Pennsylvania State University, and nearby communities, offering select works that might serve to not only to welcome newcomers through an encounter with an historic spirit of place, but also as a means to conserve and perpetuate a lively, evergreen, and affectionate attitude toward Happy Valley as a place unlike any other. Discover other Nittany Valley Press books:

The Legends of the Nittany Valley
Henry W. Shoemaker

The Pennsylvania State College 1853-1932
Erwin W. Runkle

Is Penn State a Real University?
Ben Novak

Conserving Mount Nittany
Tom Shakely

The Birth of the Craft Brew Revolution
Ben Novak

www.ingramcontent.com/pod-product-compliance
Lightning Source LLC
Chambersburg PA
CBHW060633030426
42337CB00018B/3343